WITHDRAWN
Woodridge Public Library

The History of
Robots

by Chris Oxlade

capstone

WOODRIDGE PUBLIC LIBRARY
Three Plaza Drive
Woodridge, IL 60517-5017

© 2018 Heinemann-Raintree
an imprint of Capstone Global Library, LLC
Chicago, Illinois

To contact Capstone Global Library please call 800-747-4992, or visit our website www.mycapstone.com

All rights reserved. No part of this publication may be reproduced or transmitted in any form or by any means, electronic or mechanical, including photocopying, recording, taping, or any information storage and retrieval system, without permission in writing from the publisher.

Edited by Helen Cox Cannons
Designed by Philippa Jenkins
Picture research by Svetlana Zhurkin
Production by Steve Walker
Originated by Capstone Global Library Ltd

Library of Congress Cataloging-in-Publication Data
Names: Oxlade, Chris, author.
Title: The history of robots / by Chris Oxlade.
Description: Chicago, IL : Heinemann-Raintree, 2017. | Series: Heinemann
   first library. The history of technology | Includes bibliographical
   references and index. | Audience: Ages 7-11. | Audience: Grade 2 to Grade 5.
Identifiers: LCCN 2016058452| ISBN 9781484640364 (library binding) | ISBN
   9781484640401 (pbk.) | ISBN 9781484640449 (ebook (pdf))
Subjects: LCSH: Robots—History—Juvenile literature.
Classification: LCC TJ211.2 .O868 2017 | DDC 629.8/9209—dc23
LC record available at https://lccn.loc.gov/2016058452

This book has been officially leveled by using the F&P Text Level Gradient™ Leveling System

Acknowledgments
We would like to thank the following for permission to reproduce photographs: Alamy: Interfoto, 6; Bridgeman Images: Musee d'Art et d'Histoire, Neuchatel, Switzerland/The Scribe, an automaton by Pierre Jaquet-Droz (1721-90), 1770, 7; Getty Images: AFP/Sutter General, 18, Chung Sung-Jun, 27, Corbis, 10, Imagno, 8, Ralph White, 14, SSPL, 12; NASA: JPL-Caltech/MSSS, 15; Newscom: AFLO/Rodrigo Reyes Marin, 29, AFLO/Yoshio Tsunoda, 28, Album, 9, Album/20th Century Fox, 11, EPA/Sebastian Willnow, 21, EPA/Yuri Kochetkov, 20, National Motor Museum Heritage Images, 4, Reuters/Francois Lenoir, 17, Reuters/Issei Kato, 22, Reuters/Steve Marcus, 25, ZUMA Press/Raymond Sheh, 26; Science Source: Peter Menzel, 16; Shutterstock: Andrei Kholmov, 13, Dmitry Kalinovsky, cover (right), josefkubes, cover (left), Master Video, 19, rezachka, 5, Thailand Photos for Sale, 23, Viacheslav Yakobchuk, 1; U.S. Air Force Photo by Lt. Col. Leslie Pratt, 24.

We would like to thank Matthew Anniss for his help in the preparation of this book.

Every effort has been made to contact copyright holders of any material reproduced in this book. Any omissions will be rectified in subsequent printings if notice is given to the publisher.

All the Internet addresses (URLs) given in this book were valid at the time of going to press. However, due to the dynamic nature of the Internet, some addresses may have changed, or sites may have changed or ceased to exist since publication. While the author and publisher regret any inconvenience this may cause readers, no responsibility for any such changes can be accepted by either the author or the publisher.

Printed and Bound in China
PO4603

Some words are shown in bold, **like this**. You can find out what they mean by looking in the glossary.

Modern robots were invented during the late 1950s. When you hear the word "robot" you might think of a walking machine, like a mechanical metal human! A few robots look like this, but most robots are machines that work in factories.

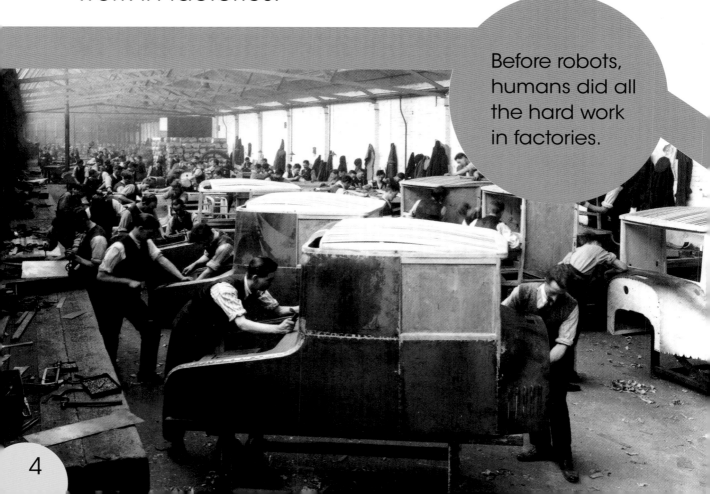

Before robots, humans did all the hard work in factories.

These factory robots are moving bricks.

Today, robots can be found in factories and homes. They are also used in hospitals, in **laboratories,** and in the sky. They carry out jobs that would be too dangerous for humans, such as **defusing** bombs.

Automatons are machines that act like humans or animals. **Complicated** systems of gears and levers move parts of their bodies. Frenchman Jacques de Vaucanson built many automatons. One of these was a lifelike duck he built in 1739.

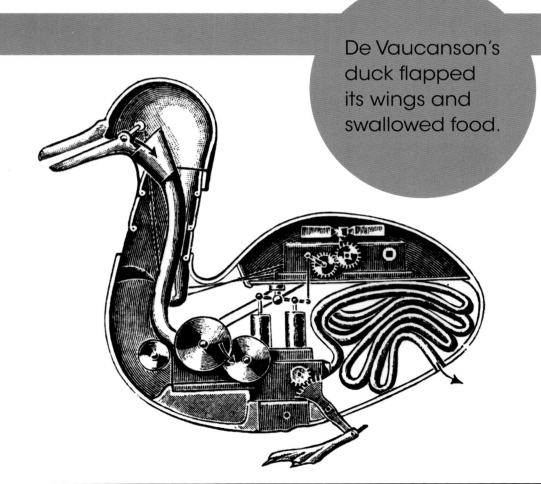

De Vaucanson's duck flapped its wings and swallowed food.

Jacquet-Droz's doll "The Scribe" was built in 1770.

In the 1760s and 1770s, Swiss watchmaker Pierre Jaquet-Droz built lifelike doll automatons. He gave them all names. Watchmakers often built automatons to show off their skills.

Storywriters imagined mechanical people long before real robots existed. In 1920, playwright Karel Capek wrote a play called *R.U.R* (Rossum's Universal Robots). It was about a scientist who creates machines that are like humans. Capek invented the word "robot."

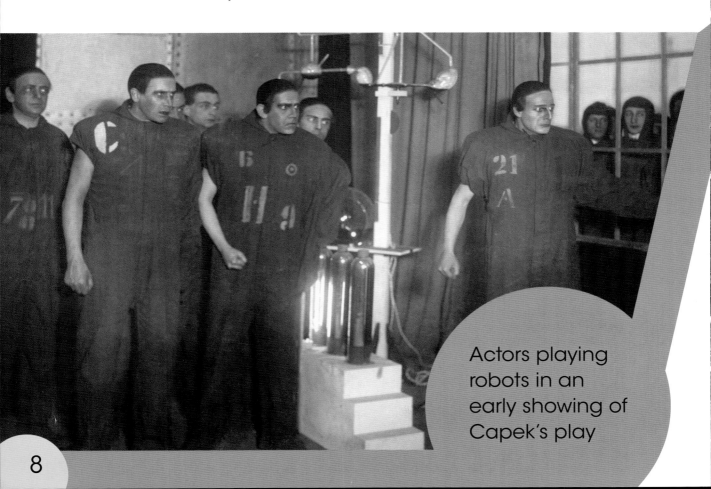

Actors playing robots in an early showing of Capek's play

Panther Science Fiction

asimov
I, Robot

Asimov's laws of robotics appeared in his book of stories called *I, Robot*.

American **science fiction** author Isaac Asimov wrote many stories about robots. In one story, Asimov wrote down three laws of **robotics**. The laws said that a robot must not harm a human, it must obey orders, and it must **protect** itself.

The idea of robots became very popular in the 1950s. There were dozens of robot stories. They were often shown in popular **science fiction** comics. Toymakers began making windup robot figures. They could walk, flash lights, and make robot noises.

Robert the Robot was a popular toy in 1959.

The film *The Day the Earth Stood Still* (1951) featured a large robot. He was called Gort.

Robots also began appearing in science fiction films. They were mostly **humanoid** robots. They were often very smart. Three famous film robots are C3-PO, R2-D2 and BB-8 from the *Star Wars* films.

Industrial robots were designed to work in factories. Most industrial robots are mechanical arms with a tool at the end. They do jobs that are too dangerous or difficult for human workers. The first industrial robot started work in 1959.

Unimate was the first industrial robot.

This factory robot is welding in a car factory.

Industrial robots were soon doing lots of different jobs. In car factories, robots lift heavy parts. They also **weld** pieces of metal together and spray paint onto cars. In other factories, they assemble tiny parts, working very **accurately**.

Robots explore places that are difficult or dangerous for humans to visit. Robot submarines called Remotely Operated Underwater Vehicles (ROVs) explore the oceans. The first ROVs dove under the sea in the 1960s.

In 1985, an ROV called *Argo* helped to find the wreck of the ship *Titanic*.

The *Curiosity* space probe landed on Mars in 2012.

Robot spacecraft are called space probes. They make long voyages to other planets and moons. They take photographs and measurements. The first successful space probe was *Luna 3*. It took photographs of the far side of the Moon in 1959.

Engineers have always been interested in building robots that can move like humans and animals. This is a big challenge. It is difficult to make robots walk and balance at the same time, especially on two legs.

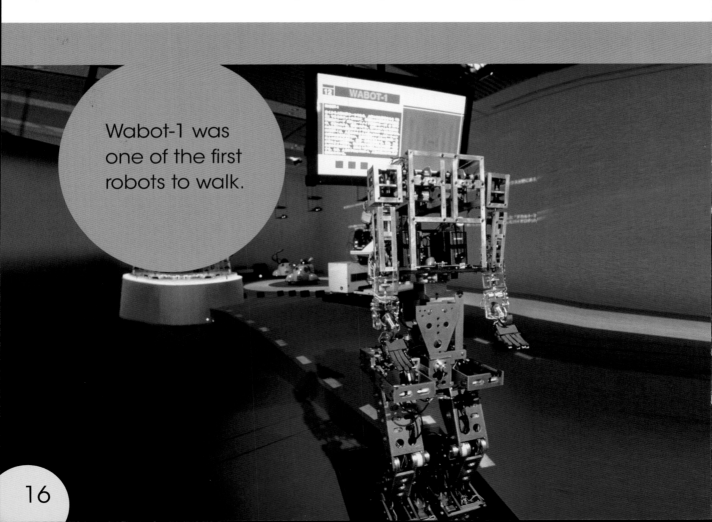

Wabot-1 was one of the first robots to walk.

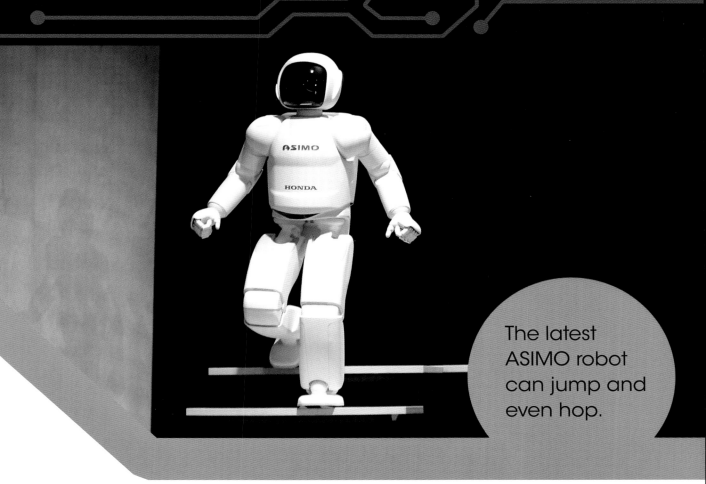

The latest ASIMO robot can jump and even hop.

In 1986, engineers at the Japanese company Honda began designing robots that could walk up and down stairs. Their first robot was the Honda P1, which was finished in 1993. In 2000, they built the robot ASIMO. ASIMO could run as well as walk.

In the 1980s, medical **surgeons** realized that robots might be able to operate on patients. In 1985, a Puma 560 **industrial** robot, controlled by a surgeon, helped with a brain operation. This was the first robotic operation.

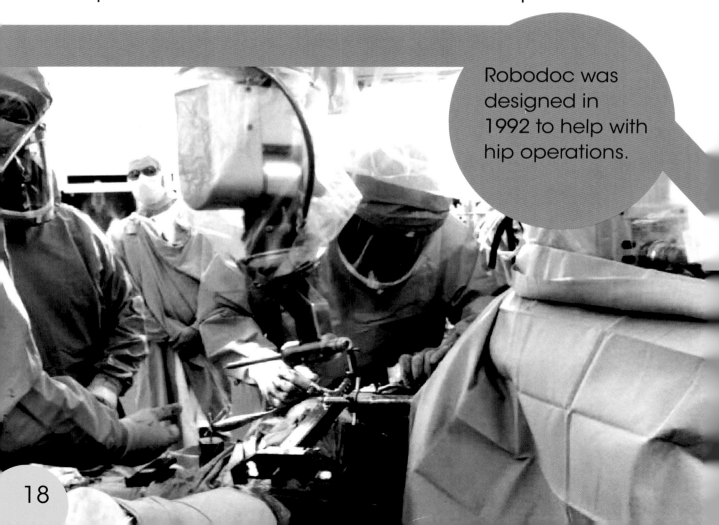

Robodoc was designed in 1992 to help with hip operations.

A surgeon watches as the da Vinci surgical robot performs an operation.

The da Vinci **surgical** robot was invented in 2000. It has performed thousands of operations. A surgeon controls da Vinci with a control unit that has a screen and stick. The surgeon can even control da Vinci remotely (from a different place).

Robotics engineers have created robots to play games and sports. They build them to learn how to make robots behave and move more skillfully. They also sometimes build them for fun!

Some robots can play chess. Robotic arms move the chess pieces.

Robots playing a game during the 2016 RoboCup

The RoboCup competition has been held every year since 1997. Teams from many different countries take part. Their robots play soccer against each other. The robots must work together as a team to win.

Domestic robots work in people's homes. Inventors have built some robot servants, but so far no robots can do all household jobs. One experimental domestic robot, called WENDY, was built at Japan's Waseda University in 1999.

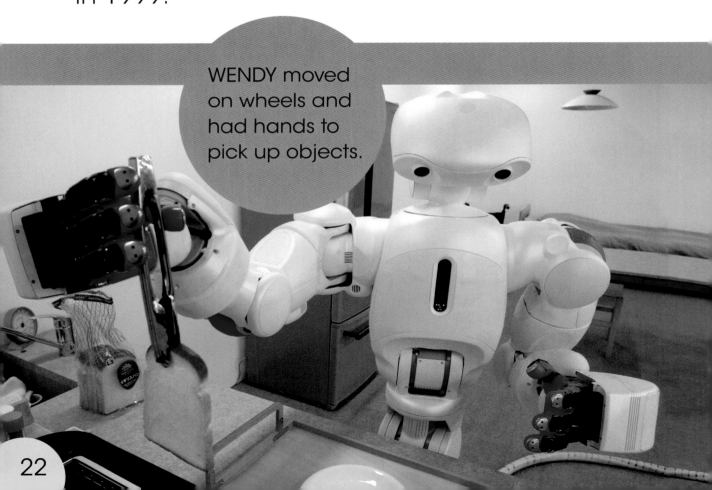

WENDY moved on wheels and had hands to pick up objects.

The Roomba vacuuming robot was first sold in 2002.

There are many domestic robots that do just one job in the home. These robots can vacuum carpets, mop floors, clean windows, and cut grass. They find their own way around and **recharge** their own batteries.

Drones are flying robots called Unmanned Aerial Vehicles (UAVs). Some drones are **remote controlled**, but others fly themselves automatically. The first drones were small military aircraft. They were used to take photographs of enemy positions.

The MQ-1 Predator drone first took off in 1994.

The Parrot AR.Drone was one of the earliest quadcopters.

A quadcopter is a small drone with four rotors that lift it into the air. A pilot flies a quadcopter from the ground using a **remote control**. The first quadcopters were developed in 2010. The latest quadcopters can send live video pictures to the pilot.

A **humanoid** robot has the same shape as a human being. It has a body, head, arms, and—sometimes—legs. **Robotics** engineers started building humanoid robots in the 1970s.

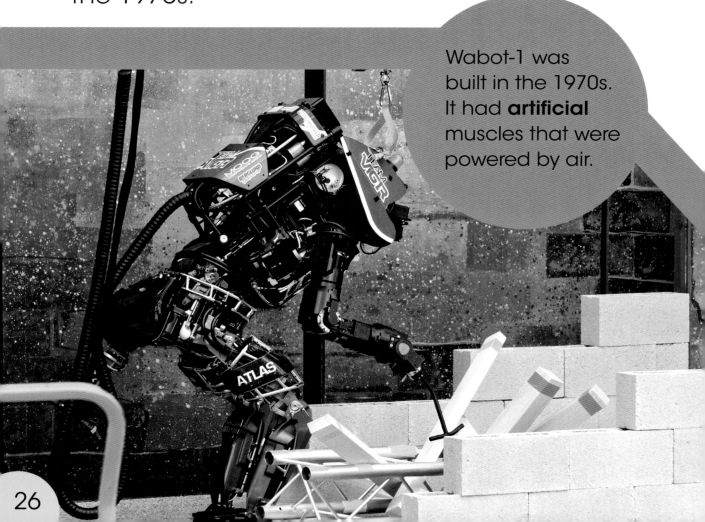

Wabot-1 was built in the 1970s. It had **artificial** muscles that were powered by air.

EveR-1 was one of the first realistic androids. It was built in 2003.

An **android** is a robot built to look like a human being. Androids have lifelike skin and faces that move. They speak and behave like humans too. Androids are becoming very realistic!

In the future, we will see more robots in our everyday lives. For example, robots that help elderly or sick people with household jobs will become more popular. But it will still be a long time before every home has a robot servant!

These home helper robots, all called Pepper, are the first to tell how humans are feeling.

In the far future, it may be difficult to tell humans and androids apart!

Robots will become more common outdoors as well. More **drones** will be in the sky, delivering packages and perhaps carrying passengers. We will also begin to see **humanoids** and **androids** in our everyday lives.

Glossary

accurate—correct in all details

android—a robot that looks like a human, with lifelike skin and a face that moves

artificial—not real

automaton—a machine that looks and moves like a human or an animal

complicated—having lots of different parts

defuse—to make a bomb safe so it will not explode

domestic—to do with the home

drone—a robotic flying machine, normally flown by remote control

humanoid—a robot that has a body, head, legs, and arms, like a human

industrial—to do with making things in factories

laboratory—a room or building used for scientific experiments or research

protect—to keep safe from harm

recharge—to put electricity into a battery, so the battery can be used again

remote control—a device for controlling something from far away

robotics—science and the study of robots

science fiction—books set in the future, all about imagined possibilities for science and technology

surgeon—a doctor who carries out operations on patients

surgical—used in surgery

weld—to join together metal parts by melting them together

Read More

Clay, Kathryn. *My First Guide to Robots*. My First Guides. North Mankato, Minn.: Capstone Press, 2015.

Stewart, Melissa. *Robots*. Washington, D.C.: National Geographic, 2014.

Tuchman, Gail. *Robots*. New York: Scholastic Inc., 2016.

Internet Sites

FactHound offers a safe, fun way to find Internet sites related to this book. All of the sites on FactHound have been researched by our staff.

Here's all you do:

Visit *www.facthound.com*

Type in this code: 9781484640364

Index

3 1524 00703 2610